W9-BPJ-353

The Most Rugged
All-Terrain
Vehicles

Jay H. Smith

Reading consultant:
John Manning, Professor of Reading
University of Minnesota

Capstone Press

C A P S T O N E   P R E S S
2440 Fernbrook Lane • Minneapolis, Minnesota 55447

Printed in the United States of America.

Library of Congress Cataloging-in-Publication Data
Smith, Jay H., 1941-
  The most rugged all terrain vehicles / by Jay H. Smith.
  p. cm. --
  Includes bibliographical references and index.
  ISBN 1-56065-218-7
  1. All terrain vehicle driving--Juvenile literature. [1. All terrain vehicle driving.] I. Title.
TL235.7.S63 1995
629.22'042--dc20

                                    94-30828
                                     CIP
                                     AC

Table of Contents

Chapter 1

Daydreams

Three years ago, you saw a video that made a lasting impression on you. It was about all-**terrain** vehicles, or ATVs. It seemed these strange-looking vehicles could go anywhere and carry just about anything. They were tough and practical–but they also looked like fun.

Since then, another video has been playing over and over in your imagination. You picture yourself cruising through the woods on your own ATV. You cross rushing streams and churn through muddy swamps. Jagged rocks and fallen trees block your path, but you run right over them.

You bounce through thick brush and across shifting sands. The ATV seems to take no notice of the ruts and **whoops** on the trail. Finally, at the end of the ride, you **clean a hill** as the vehicle's momentum carries you up and over the top.

Now your daydreams are coming true. You have finally saved enough money to buy a good used ATV and all the safety gear you need. That equipment, your **common sense**, and a good training course should make ATV riding as fun as you have imagined.

ATV racers need skill and endurance to compete on rough terrain.

Chapter 2

What's an ATV?

There are many ways to describe an ATV. One expert explains that it's "a motorcycle with four wheels." Another says, "An ATV is a four-wheeled dirt bike that looks a little like a riding lawn mower." Still another thinks an ATV is "a cross between a motorcycle and a dune buggy."

You get the idea. An ATV does have much in common with a motorcycle. Both vehicles have the same types of motors and the same operating controls. And riders of ATVs and motorcycles sit and steer the same way.

A steep hill can launch a speeding ATV into a big jump. Just make sure you have a clear spot to land.

Major Differences

There are, however, major differences between the two machines. ATVs, of course, have more wheels. The earliest ATVs had six wheels, but all ATVs now have four wheels.

Motorcycles and ATVs also handle differently. ATVs ride closer to the ground and are more stable. The tires of an ATV are wider, and their air pressure is lower. These studded tires, also called **knobbies**, can take shocks that would flatten a motorcycle tire.

Most important of all, ATVs can ride on all kinds of terrain in all kinds of weather. When snow begins to fall, and roads and trails get slippery, motorcycles must be put away for the season. ATVs keep right on going.

ATVs continue to grow in popularity. Yamaha, a Japanese company, used to sell far more motorcycles than ATVs. But now ATVs make up 60 percent of Yamaha's sales.

Knobbies can handle mud, rocks, and heavy impacts that would flatten ordinary motorcycle tires.

Six Fat Tires on a Bathtub

ATVs were invented in Canada in the late 1950s. By the early 1970s, there were more than 50,000 of them in the United States and Canada. Many farmers and ranchers used these early ATVs to herd cattle and sheep.

The machines were also useful for carrying heavy equipment over rough terrain. Most of the early ATVs were six-wheelers. Some people described them as "six fat tires on a bathtub."

By the early 1980s, very few six-wheelers remained. The three-wheeler had replaced them. Many people used three-wheeled ATVs on camping trips or for riding on dirt trails. Some raced them in competitions.

The Three-Wheeler

The three-wheeled ATV could also be dangerous. On a curve or hill, a careless driver could easily flip over. These accidents caused many injuries and even some deaths.

People became alarmed by ATV accidents. The Consumer Products Safety Commission, a

government agency, threatened to take action against companies that made ATVs. By 1988, ATV manufacturers agreed to stop selling three-wheelers. They also agreed to set new **guidelines**. The guidelines were meant to stop children from driving four-wheeled ATVs that were too big for them.

Suzuki Introduces the Quad

Suzuki introduced the first four-wheeler in 1985. The **quad** was an instant success. It was more stable and less dangerous than the three-wheelers.

Safety is still important in the ATV industry. All of the major manufacturers–the Japanese "big four" of Honda, Kawasaki, Suzuki, and Yamaha, and the U.S. company Polaris–offer customers videos on how to ride safely. They also give **rebates** if you complete a training course after buying an ATV.

The Suzuki Quad–a four-wheeled all-terrain vehicle–first came out in 1985.

Chapter 3

Getting Started

Once you have decided to try ATV riding, you need to find the right machine. When buying a new or used ATV, you should consider your age, your weight and body size, your skill level, and how you will be using the vehicle.

Your Age

The youngest ATV riders should start with small ATVs–those with engines no larger than 70 cubic centimeters (4.3 cubic inches). There are not too many choices at this size. A good one is the Italjet Coyote 50.

Riders between 12 and 15 years old should use an ATV of 90 cubic centimeters (5.5 cubic inches) or less. The Suzuki LT80 QuadSport and the Yamaha YFM80 are good choices in this category.

Riders 16 and over can choose larger ATVs. They should carefully consider their weight and body size before doing so. An ATV that is too large for its driver can be dangerous.

Your Riding Needs

Choose an ATV that does what you really need it to do. There are different machines for recreational use, for farm work, and for racing. Lighter ATVs are great for a day of trail-riding on fairly level terrain. There are also tough, durable vehicles that can stand up to heavy use day after day. Jack Jensen of the Lazy J Ranch in Clovis, California, owns one of these.

Every day of the year, Jack uses his ATV for work on his ranch. "My Four Trax 250X acts

Even when they're airborne, good ATV riders keep their eyes on the trail ahead.

as my horse, truck, and patrol vehicle," he says. He has even used his ATV for guarding his property during a range war.

Other Factors

If you are a young adult just starting out in the sport, your build and your weight are still important.

Beginners should ride an entry-level machine, such as a **two-stroke** ATV that is smaller than 200 cubic centimeters (12.2 cubic inches), or a **four-stroke** ATV under 250 cubic centimeters (15.3 cubic inches).

It's foolish to buy a lot of extra power that you won't be able to use. As your riding skills improve, you can move up to the more powerful models used by experienced riders.

Two-Stroke or Four-Stroke Engines

In choosing an ATV, you must also consider the type of engine you want. Two-stroke engines are less expensive and easier to rebuild and repair than the four-strokes. In addition,

two-strokes are lighter and have fewer moving parts than four-strokes.

Four-stroke engines, on the other hand, are heavier, quieter, and more reliable. They are also more powerful and can run longer without an engine rebuild.

The two-stroke engine burns a mixture of gas and oil. Because this fuel causes a lot of air pollution, some riders prefer four-stroke ATVs. Instead of gasoline, some two-stroke riders use ethanol, which burns cleaner.

Used ATVs

If you have a small budget, it might be a good idea to buy a used ATV. There are bargains to be found, if you know what model and size you need. Ask an experienced rider to check out the vehicle *before* you buy.

Riding Areas

It's against the law to ride ATVs on public roads, so you'll need to find an off-road area or trail to use. This can be difficult, especially if

you live in a big city. You may have to haul the vehicle a long distance to reach a suitable spot.

Check with your ATV dealer for information on ATV trails in your area. Or join an ATV club. The club will have information on the best local riding spots.

Chapter 4

Safety

Safety is the most important part of having fun on your ATV. Remembering some basic safety tips will help you get the most out of your vehicle. Some states require you to take a safety or training course. Even if your state does not require a course, the training will improve your riding skills.

ATV Safety Institute

The ATV Safety Institute (ASI) offers courses all over the country. Experienced ASI instructors will teach you about pre-ride inspections, warmup exercises, braking, turning, and shifting. You will learn about clutch and throttle control, about the importance of body position and **body English**, and about simple maintenance.

ASI instructors also cover riding techniques and how to tackle obstacles, hills, and different kinds of trails. Finally, they show ATV riders how to avoid damage to the environment.

To find the ASI course nearest you, call (800) 447-4700. A few states require organizations other than ASI to lead the training.

Safety Gear

The more safety gear you have, the more fun you will have. Flashy or expensive equipment is unnecessary. All you need is good, sturdy gear that will reduce the risk of injury. Be prepared–accidents do happen.

Without the right safety gear, a wild ride can turn into a dangerous crash.

You *absolutely* need a helmet, boots, goggles, and a shirt with long sleeves. Young people under 16 need more protection.

Here is what is recommended:

helmet–a good, full-face helmet

goggles–for keeping out dirt and sand

jersey–the best are long-sleeved with elbow pads

gloves–best with finger and knuckle guards

chest protector/shoulder pads–best with elbow and full back protection

kidney belt–to hold your back and stomach firmly

knee protectors–to guard against painful injury

riding pants–motocross pants with hip and thigh pads

boots–motocross boots are best

Use Your Head

You can keep safe by using your head. *Think* while you ride. Always watch carefully for problems and dangers. Remember, **hotdogging** is for fools.

These tips will help you ride smart.

- Never operate an ATV unless you have been properly instructed.

- Do not try to ride beyond your ability.

- Inspect your ATV before riding. Check all controls, as well as steering, lights, and tires.

- Practice often on level surfaces before moving up to tougher terrain.

- Do not follow directly behind another rider. It's harder to see what's ahead.

- Quads can easily spin out. Practice leaning into turns.

- On frozen lakes or rivers, look out for thin ice.

- When going downhill, carefully select the line most free of obstacles. Then stay with it all the way down.

- Never carry a passenger on your ATV.

- Never ride alone.

- All hills are different. Be ready to make adjustments.

- When you ride through water, look out for submerged rocks and dropoffs.

- Carry a repair kit and a first-aid kit with you.

- Always show courtesy to other riders and respect for the rules of the road.

- Get to know what your ATV can and cannot do.

Chapter 5

Moving Up to Racing

After you have spent many practice hours on your ATV, you may decide to try racing. There are competitions for amateurs and for professionals, for all age levels, and for all models of ATVs.

ATV races include cross-country, motocross, flat track, and TT (Tourist Trophy) courses. There are even ice races during the winter.

ATV racers are serious about the rules of their sport. Pre-race safety inspections are

A racing ATV swims through a watery obstacle.

Smooth, frozen tracks provide a fast surface for cold weather courses.

tough. Vehicles and their riders have to meet high standards.

An ATV Superstar

Gary Denton, of Chino, California, has been called the Michael Jordan of ATV racing. Now in his mid-30s, Gary is older than most riders on the ATV-racing circuit. Some people say

that he is the best rider there has ever been. He is most famous for his fast starts. He breaks away from the rest of the field in a technique known as **hole-shotting.**

Gary's skill has earned him seven straight Grand National Championships. In the first Grand National Championship TT race of the 1994 season, at Greenville, Tennessee, Gary won by a big margin.

In Mickey Thompson stadium racing, Greg Stuart, Mark Ehrhardt, Joe Byrd, Charlie Shepherd, Nic Granlund, Doug Eichner, and Gary Denton are the superstars. Eichner won the 1993 Mickey Thompson Gran Prix.

The leading ATV motocross riders are Doug Gust and Gary Denton. The superstars of cross-country (scrambles) are Bob Sloan, Barry Hawk, and Steve Holbert. In the fourth round of the 1994 National Cross-Country Championship at Brownsville, Pennsylvania, Holbert won over Hawk.

Paris-Dakar Rally

Perhaps the toughest racing event in all of motor sports is the Paris-Dakar Rally. This is an incredible test that is 3,500 miles (5,632.7 kilometers) long. The course runs round-trip between Paris, France, and Dakar in the African nation of Senegal. Much of the course follows rugged desert terrain.

Several ATV riders have entered the Paris-Dakar Rally. Before 1994, no ATV rider ever got as far as Senegal. But in that year Frederic Fourgeaud rode on a Polaris Big Boss 4x6 350. It took this French rider a week to reach Dakar. This was too slow to qualify for the return trip to Paris. But his performance was the best yet for an ATV in the Paris-Dakar.

Glossary

amateur–someone who is not a professional

body English–movement of the body to control and maneuver a vehicle

clean a hill–to soar over the top of a hill

common sense–good judgment that cannot be taught

entry-level–beginning; something for beginners

four-stroke engine–a type of engine that completes one power cycle every four piston strokes. Most four-stroke ATVs are cooled by air.

guidelines–a set of policies or rules

hole-shotting–a technique used to take the lead at the start of an ATV race

hotdogging–showing off with unusual maneuvers

knobbies–wide, studded tires

quad–a four-wheeled ATV

rebate–return of some of the money used to buy something

terrain–characteristics of the land

two-stroke engine–an engine that completes one power cycle every two piston strokes. Most new two-stroke ATVs are liquid-cooled and have no cooling fins on the cylinder.

whoops–a series of jumps from five to ten feet (1.5 to 3 meters) apart and one to three feet (.3 to 1 meter) high

Acknowledgments

Special thanks to John Arens of *Dirt Wheels* magazine, Bill Lanphier of *3 & 4 Wheel Action* magazine, and Dan Cunningham.

To Learn More

Estrem, Paul. *ATVs*. Mankato, MN: Crestwood
House, 1987.

Maddock, Bobby. *First to the Flag in an ATV*.
Fort Lauderdale, FL: Maddock Racing Press,
1984.

Malo, John W. *All-Terrain Adventure Vehicles*.
New York: Macmillan, 1972.

You can read about ATVs in these magazines:
Dirt Wheels, Cycle World, and *3 & 4 Wheel
Action.*

Photo Credits:
All photographs courtesy of John Arens and Jim
Talkington.

Index